FORESTS

A Buddy Book
by
Fran Howard

ABDO
Publishing Company

VISIT US AT

www.abdopublishing.com

Published by ABDO Publishing Company, 4940 Viking Drive, Edina, Minnesota 55435.

Copyright © 2007 by Abdo Consulting Group, Inc. International copyrights reserved in all countries. No part of this book may be reproduced in any form without written permission from the publisher. Buddy Books™ is a trademark and logo of ABDO Publishing Company.

Printed in the United States.

Edited by: Sarah Tieck
Contributing Editor: Michael P. Goecke
Graphic Design: Brady Wise
Image Research: Deb Coldiron, Maria Hosley, Heather Sagisser, Brady Wise
Photographs: Eyewire, Flat Earth, Michael P. Goecke, Photodisc, photos.com

Library of Congress Cataloging-in-Publication Data

Howard, Fran, 1953-
    Forests / Fran Howard.
        p. cm. — (Habitats)
    Includes bibliographical references and index.
    ISBN 1-59679-777-0 (10 digit ISBN)
    ISBN 978-1-59679-777-2 (13 digit ISBN)
        1. Forests—Juvenile literature. I. Title. II. Series: Habitats (Edina, Minn.)

QH86.H67 2006
577.3—dc22

                                                                2005031596

TABLE OF CONTENTS

WHAT IS A FOREST?

Trees help clean the air. They also make oxygen for people to breathe.

Forests are land areas covered with trees. There are many smaller plants. There are mosses and flowers that live in forests, too.

A forest is one kind of habitat. Habitats are the places where plants and animals find food, water, and places to live. Different plants and animals live in different habitats.

Most of the world's plants and animals live in forests. They need sunlight and water to grow.

Moss and other small plants grow in forests, too.

WHERE ARE FORESTS FOUND?

Today, it is estimated that forests cover about one-third of the land on Earth. Forests grow in many places around the world.

Forests have several layers. Different plants and animals live in each layer of the forest.

A few of the tallest trees form a layer. It is called the emergent layer. This layer is closest to the sun.

Just below, the tops of the trees form a thick covering called a **canopy**. Birds and monkeys often live in the canopy.

A parrot is one bird that lives in the canopy.

Under the **canopy** is the understory. The understory includes small trees that are not tall enough for the canopy. The shrub layer is next. Shrubs and plants grow there.

Rabbits live in the forest.

A view of the shrub layer.

The grasshopper is one insect that lives on the forest floor.

The forest floor is the lowest layer. Life begins on the forest floor. Rotting leaves, twigs, and needles cover the forest floor. Worms and tiny insects eat the rotting plants. These rotting plants turn into soil. The soil helps the trees grow.

LAYERS OF A FOREST

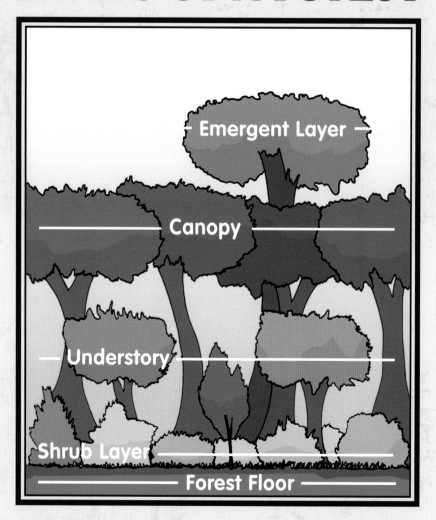

Emergent Layer

Canopy

Understory

Shrub Layer

Forest Floor

DIFFERENT
TYPES OF FORESTS

There are many different forests around the world. The three main types of forests include the boreal forest, the temperate forest, and the tropical forest. Different animals and plants live in each one.

The boreal forest grows in the northern part of the world. Usually, it is found in cold places. There are boreal forests in the United States, Canada, Scandinavia, and Russia.

Temperate forests grow in places with mild temperatures. Temperate forests change during the different seasons of the area they are in. There are temperate forests in North America, Asia, and Europe.

Tropical forests grow in hot, rainy places. There are tropical forests in Africa, Central America, Australia, and Asia.

A boreal forest in Alberta, Canada.

A temperate forest in Finland.

A tropical forest in Ecuador.

LIFE IN THE BOREAL FOREST

Needles grow on conifers.

Most of the trees that grow in boreal forests are called **conifers**. These trees have needles instead of leaves. They grow well in cool weather.

Seeds grow in the cones of a conifer.

Conifers keep their needles all year. These trees are also called evergreens. Spruce and fir trees are conifers. Conifer trees have cones.

Many different animals live in the boreal forest. There are worms, birds, and moose. There are also woodchucks, mice, and squirrels. Foxes, owls, and lynx all live in this forest, too.

Wolves live in the boreal forest.

LIFE IN THE TEMPERATE FOREST

Buds grow into leaves.

The temperate forest has many **deciduous** trees. Deciduous trees shed their leaves each year during the autumn. In the spring, buds form on the twigs.

17

Chlorophyll makes leaves green.
Chlorophyll helps plants make food from sunlight.

In spring and summer, most leaves are green. In autumn, the leaves turn red or yellow. Then, they die and fall off the tree.

Fall leaves are colorful.

At the end of autumn, all the leaves drop off the tree branches.

19

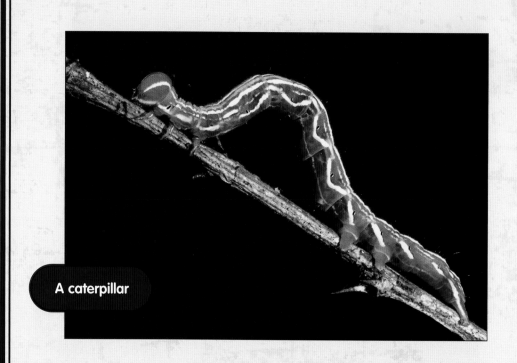

A caterpillar

Many different animals live in the temperate forest. There are caterpillars, squirrels, mice, and chipmunks. Raccoons, foxes, and black bears also live in this forest.

A chipmunk

A squirrel

A fox

A black bear cub

21

LIFE IN THE TROPICAL FOREST

Toucans live in the tropical forest.

Tropical forests are warm and **humid**. The rain forest is one kind of tropical forest. Many plants and animals live in the rain forest.

Banana trees can be found in tropical forests. It rains almost every day in some tropical forests. This helps plants grow quickly.

A tree frog

Rain forests have more types of trees than any other forest. Most of these trees stay green all year. They have big leaves. The **canopy** is very **dense**. The floor of the rain forest is very dark. The leaves rot quickly there.

The Amazon Rain Forest is one of the largest tropical rain forests in the world. The Amazon Rain Forest makes about 20 percent of the oxygen for the world.

Hoffman's two-toed sloth

Many animals live in the tropical forest. The **canopy** is full of colorful birds such as parrots. Sloths spend most of their time in the canopy eating leaves. Monkeys also play and eat in the canopy. Termites and other insects eat the rotting leaves and wood on the ground.

A howler monkey

Howler monkeys howl each morning.
The **canopy** is a noisy place.

WHY ARE FOREST HABITATS IMPORTANT?

People and animals need forests. Trees make air that people and animals breathe. Some forest plants supply medicine.

People use trees to make many products. They make lumber and paper. People also cut down forests to grow crops. Sometimes people cut down too many trees.

Forest animals and plants need each other. Together they form a **food chain**. Even the smallest plants and animals are part of a food chain.

Plants and animals of the forest cannot live without their habitat.

Lynx   Snowshoe Hare   Twigs

FORESTS

- The world's largest tree is the General Sherman Tree. It is 274 feet (84 m) tall. Its trunk is about 37 feet (11 m) wide. It is found in Sequoia National Forest in California. This tree is more than 2,000 years old.

- People can tell how old a tree is by looking at its trunk. To find out the tree's exact age, scientists look at the rings on its stump. Each ring represents one year.

- Maple syrup comes from the forest. It is made from the sap of sugar maple trees.

- The Rafflesia is the world's largest flower. It can be three feet (one m) wide. It is found in the tropical forest of Borneo.

- Some birds and squirrels bury seeds to eat later. These seeds often grow into new trees.

IMPORTANT WORDS

canopy a shelter over the forest formed by the treetops.

conifer an evergreen tree that produces cones.

deciduous trees that shed their leaves each year.

dense having many things in a small area.

food chain the order in which plants and animals feed on each other.

humid air that is warm or damp.

WEB SITES

Would you like to learn more about **forests**? Please visit ABDO Publishing Company on the World Wide Web to find Web site links about **forests**. These links are routinely monitored and updated to provide the most current information available.

www.abdopublishing.com

INDEX